POETRY

POETRY

*UEA Postgraduate
Creative Writing Anthology
2018*

CONTENTS

TIFFANY ATKINSON
Foreword

Suddenly, I realise that a year – maybe more – has gone by in which not once have I heard anyone talk about poetry's supposed marginality or 'irrelevance'. Such conversations had become a commonplace of my writing life. What changed? Was it something in poetry – perhaps the international and genre-bending success of recent experimental collections like Claudia Rankine's *Citizen: An American Lyric* (2014) or Ocean Vuong's *Night Sky With Exit Wounds* (2016) – or could it be that notions of marginality and significance are shifting in the value systems of culture at large? One can only hope. Of course poets themselves have never bought into the whole irrelevance thing. What could be more timely than the wresting of new ways of saying from the hand-me-down matter of language; what more exploratory and exacting/exciting? Perhaps, in an era of frequently cynical and lazy language-use, an appetite has grown among readers for writing that doesn't so much hit the nail squarely on the head, as refashion the very concept of the hammer.

And it is this putting of things otherwise, in patterns and shapes that resist habituated expression and reading habits, that perhaps most strikingly distinguishes poetry from prose. Poetry thus asks for a certain care and slowness in reading, since speed-reading and summary is not the point, and no poem expects you to hurry. Poetry evangelist that I am, I would claim a value and relevance in this experience, too: that of being momentarily and pleasurably adrift in a fresh linguistic environment. Seen in this light, each poem is not simply an exercise of wresting the author's perception or opinion into a neat verbal container; rather, the poem becomes itself, as poet and critic Lyn Hejinian has put it, 'the field of enquiry', a space in which the poet experiments with what it is possible to say and do in language.[1] And we are better, more imaginative readers than we think. You can hold up a poem in front of a class of ten year olds, and even if they can't see the words they will make sense of the pattern it makes on the page, the dialogue between blocks of utterance and silence. There is a kind of speculative play at work in this kind of reading, so different from our normal reading lives.

1 Lyn Hejinian, *The Language of Inquiry* (University of California Press, 2001)

If this is something that strikes the reader, how much more powerful this effect for the writer, who often opens their blank page or screen with little or no idea of what kind of pattern, what kind of formal demand may emerge. If I write prose I may simply write sentences that run to the margin and then continue to the end of the page, much as if I were opening my mouth to speak. If I write a poem I feel more like a painter with brush in hand, who approaches the blank canvas and must decide to make some kind of mark that says: Here, this, here is something happening, now something is being expressed where before there was nothing, and with each line-break this exploratory process begins anew. I think this is what Lyn Hejinian means when she says, 'I turn to the line in order to begin', perhaps as Wassily Kandinsky once described drawing as 'taking a line for a walk.' A line may be many things: a unit of utterance or thought, a measure, a persuasion, a breath, a transatlantic connection, a trap, a song-line, a sight-line, a flight, a fingerprint, a musical phrase, a hit. A poem is a pressurised accumulation of these working parts, a whole new engine of thought, or an ecosystem. And goodness knows, we need more of those.

An anthology of emerging poets, then, is perhaps the purest accumulation of new beginnings. This volume is the record of a year of hard work, experiment, conversation, revision, and speculative play between the weight of tradition and the desire to find new ways of saying. What is immediately visible in these pages is the sheer variation in style and form, from the fragmentary and epigrammatic to the ranging and discursive, from the intimate to the global, from the playful to the elegiac. What is not visible is the mutual care and camaraderie of a group working together to encourage the emergence of each distinctive voice, so I mention that now as one of the many joys and privileges of being part of this process. Here are the poets of 2018. Remember, you saw them here first.

Tiffany Atkinson
UEA
May 2018

This diverse anthology comprises the latest work from the 2018 cohort of poets studying UEA's renowned Creative Writing MA.

Gboyega Abayomi-Odubanjo is a British-Nigerian poet born and raised in East London. Prior to his MA in Poetry, he completed a BA in English Literature and Philosophy at the University of East Anglia.

If I Could Travel to Any Place and Any Time I Would

go to bed   with all the strangers who got my name right and party
like it was 1999 or 5pm somewhere in the empire

    i would drink jesus dry
watch me i would   ask for the most expensive stuff
i've already asked for so many things   so i probably wouldn't have asked

if everybody started breaking stuff
    probably would have just broken stuff   as well
would have made sure that i got a big new telly

    during the riots in 2011
a man on the news is heard saying free nelson mandela   innit
    and i bet that he would   climb the prison gates himself

i bet he would try   love winnie himself i bet he would try
kiss babies sing freedom and happy i bet that he would

Eating Good

i used to want a seat
at the table where
they've got the name
branded juices. i used to
want every breakfast
that the happy families
on tv start but don't finish.
pray that the smell of
mum's cooking don't cling
to school collar. pray
i could play out
on halloween
that daddy didn't shoo away
the pagans
with names off of
coca-cola bottles. i used to
pray for blue eyes
and cooties but now all i want
is to be fela kuti. now every
body on tv is foreign
we *as-salamu alaykum* in public
we're bathing with buckets. now it's
two thousand and something

i'm still talking about this.
we on nigerian timing.
now in my gaff there's no
seat there's no table. we eat
with our hands. we darker than blue.
now in my gaff there's no seat
but we eating. no table
but still we are eating.

Watershed

we were told
to stay off the music channels
but when michael sang ma makoosa
we found ourselves fingering
bass with mtv louded up
soft carpet on toes headbanging
with afros as close to the telly as possible
went looking for cds our parents kept
in cabinets
found them

Swimming

and so over ocean
hoping we go
weathered by a toneless
sky grey /
mulatto. i let my spine
be your deck and i stroke.
the clothes from my back /
your flag. you stand
pointing new world. i stroke.
listen to you promising
ocean good blue.
i stroke i stroke slow
you promise stone into bread
water from stone
into water we go
your voice it goes on
but there's water in throat
and there's water
i stroke and there's water
we're drowning and i
as a boy could not swim
still i stroke. your voice
now a nothing
the water it sings
and we're drowning
i stroke.

Money Dance

look at them on friday—saturday night

                before god come and clean them good

look the way their face sweating

         so that when you press that note on their forehead it

sticks for just a little while then shimmy

         down—you never see nothing like it not anywhere

the way that palm wine fill them 'til their belly full

           look at the money fall look at the way it falls

like problems falling away look at the way

            they dance like problems falling away

look

YOU WANT JAZZ, WE GOT THAT fatman jazz
        that cocked hat no welcome mat that room
    full of chapped-lipped scallywags drunk
      on fermented marula fruit jazz
          strummed with six-
              fingered hands jazz
          tap dancing doused
                  in one million
          by paco rabanne
    eating with our feet type of jazz
          glory to the black jesus jazz
type of jazz they've got at segregated parties
          that popped blood vessel screeching   tired
                          and black
                      as pots and kettles
                                  the jazz is too loud
              that open collar
                  and slow inco
              herence jazz
                  another name
              for a   god
          you'll   never   know
          type of   jazz
                      that jazz jazz,
                          fatman jazz

Naomi Afrassiabi is a poet with a rare and special confusion. She is based in London. Although writing is her primary focus, she is involved with various music projects which are most often concerned with the same themes as her poetry.

this poetry is so healthy
so i really want to like it

little gherkin girl

body wrapped each other
warped in curtains
wrapping
windows which are
cold wrapped

by fogs and moist
draw me a face
on window there
here waiting
wanting

face to be wrapped in breath blown on
that warped window naked wrapped
in clothes which rasp and
i am pickled

in you
you taste so strong and
your bite
marks are so distinctive
they will find and arrest
you soon water is rarely still despite
its label
and it's all your fault for shaking the tin
your gherkin

will go to the cinema to see you in 3D glasses
which don't suit it sometimes it wishes it could
enjoy porn
and had a cock because its shape is the same but
it can't

cram itself into vaginas it would get lost it is
too small
and too green and no one is willing and
its brine
pours over the edges of its container
and falls
everywhere and it dies in a pool of brine

and blood and the water that
makes up 98%
of its being is NOT still and i take it
and put it in my pocket so
it knows what

it is to be naked but wrapped in clothes
still but naked still

but really,

you're a piece of shit and

i know you are desperate

to metabolise my vagina

something dying inside you
and you feel it worm dies and
releases poisonous decay and
you feel it and have a sudden
blinding headache it becomes
clear that you have lost him but
you continue with pride and
serious endeavour to

harbour the sexually parasitic

i am desperate to express that,

i need you to come here and purify me
because i am so congested and you
are like witch hazel so fresh and so clean
maybe you have the ability to exfoliate me
really well so that all the death and dirt is
rubbed away and i am purely yours and
beautiful in a very specific kind of way
something like a photoshopped catalogue
of scandinavian furniture which is all based
on some wipe-down easy-to-live-with practicality
because we all know or some of us do that
morality is practical for some people and not
for others but i am willing to adhere to your kind of
clean and not problem-skin morality despite any
hormonal changes i want to be polished by you
with a hard but natural and environmentally friendly
sponge we could keep a wooden back brush in our
shower room and i'd pay for my own wax don't
worry this bit is not about that feminism i know that
hair also makes you smell and sometimes things can
even live in it but i just want to be with you and no
other things and i hope that i can do it i hope that i do
not make any mistakes and i am very careful with sugar
i think it will be ok i love capers very much especially the
big ones and i think that they are fair trade and so juicy so
we don't even need to juice them or anything we could just
suck them and stare into each other's clear white post-
cucumbered eyes and say i love you baby i really hope
that you can save me from the dirt between my toes
i have been doing yoga to try and practise for
when we start to be in love but i cannot reach them
still except with a very long qtip oh plz love me you have
such straight lines where the barber cut the border of
your face and it is so sexually attractive especially in the
sense that i know your penis would taste exactly like
nothing and then exactly like pineapple you are some kind
of spa god that wanders clean streets and lies in whiteness

i love you so much please take me to indonesia

oh and,

i am very sticky between my fingers (dirty) because i picked up sugar
(it's so hard to write a taste) with them it feels weird on silver

rings i have oats on my gums and
am chewing

them cinnamon is dissolving near the back of my throat i rub
my tongue on my gums inside my mouth and once

(more times over more time)

over my lips my foot feels almost numb because i'm sitting
on it and i almost always do there (see)

are two *pressures* on either side of my spine

maybe it is muscle building or maybe it's just ligaments bending out

of whack I'm not sure my eyes feel as they do the way i live with them
sometimes i close one for a while to see better but i am not doing that now
i feel neither weak nor strong i want to have sex all the time but not really
just sometimes it feels like that like right now   and now   and now

tongue so tiny like a pink oat same colour as fresh pink gum and nipples
are blueberries I'm sorry we couldn't spend more time together i also
    wanted to
but this isn't the place and there wasn't any

for (.)

you are hot and i
fancy you but i
told all your friends
and all my friends
i didn't because i
was embarrassed
about being such a
slut and fancying so
many people even
though our circles
are pretty fine with
that kind of behaviour
and accepting i don't
think they are that much
and i obviously have
internalised some bad
things or something i do
fancy you though i really
liked how you had sex
with me and you grabbed
my ass cheeks and bounced
me around it was really
special no one fucks
like that people are generally
scared on the first time
round and i definitely came
i don't know why i stop talking
to anyone now unless
i'm their favourite but
i can't handle it i suppose
even though i say that
its really true that i don't
get jealous that's true
i guess it's a different
feeling like boredom that
it's not instantly love and
we'll run away to somewhere or
some bullshit what's wrong
with me you are cute anyway
is what i would say if i could

and i suppose i might say
anyway sometime when i'm
drunk on the road and walking
home and then you appear
out of nowhere and we are
finally alone together it's just
all a bit complicated and i
could text you this but i could
text five other people this too
except i'd have to edit out the
bit about the fucking because
that was honestly special and rare

bloody bloody bloody hell week sorry but
a good friend called me monday and recommended a podcast
he said *you live under a heavy, dirty, mossy, wet*
rock under droopy, greying, sloppy, brutal
skies. perspective is important everything's
changing all of our friends' names are
different, susan is robbie and, jane is ed and, liam is gorgonzola death squad
    band names awful, and,
due to disappearing distances,
has moved very far away

i respond that *please trust me i know that*
and i don't want you to hate me because
i enjoyed that blockade that time but i need
you to know that

i'm a-political
but politicised purely because of my body.
purely because of my body so fleshy and my voice and it will get
better,

because the world is only finite
and my iridescence is only finite and

                    this is only finite

Blythe Zarozinia Aimson is a poet from the Peak District, currently based in Norwich, who uses the lyric voice to explore queerness, the uncanny, and natural phenomena. Her work can be found in *Volta: An Obscurity of Poets*, *Occulum* Journal, and HVTN.

sail needle

i was told
when a sailor dies they're sewn up
in their own hammock

        that the last stitch on his winding sheet
        goes through the bottom lip
        a tongue pillar pierced with cord

                just to check

and not   throw them overboard
trussed in canvas
still living

but an ex-navy man said
it's the law of the sea
that it's the nose   not lip

i wonder which nostril
or if it's the septum
        for the sake of symmetry

common stinging nettle
urtica dioica

nettles aren't cruel even tho
they sting with hairs that exude

> formic acid
> histamine

this is a protective feature

they will heal my burns in a poultice
calm my gingivitis
flush out urinary tract infections which
i discovered can be caused by
flavoured condoms
which are not designed for vaginal intercourse

urtica promotes hair growth i should
grow more body hair and learn to
exude acid

even i am not masochistic enough
to become a competitive   nettle eater or self
flagellate with two metre long stalks i'm
a brat in that respect would
rather just be
slapped

ginger and rosehips

zingiber officinale and rosa canina

ginger is known
for quelling nausea   and relieving cramps
but also tends to make bleeding
heavier   this is why

i add rosehips to ginger tea
they are good for menstruation induced anaemia
it's all the iron   the best hips

are from dog roses
after a frost   not dog rose
as in canine but dog as in *dagge*
as in dagger but still
they are called *rosa canina*

meaning 'pleasure and pain'
and i am susceptible   too much belly   soft skin
would like to be pricked

Craig Barker spent his year in Norwich teaching the English language, learning Mandarin, selling furniture, and writing poetry. The majority of said poetry was about the first dog in space, but he decided against submitting anything too sad. He regrets nothing. You can find him online at www.craigwritesthings.com

Daughters (Short Version)

Woke up to find five names in the margins,
        unknown scrawls gaining clarity
as the sunlight split the wallpaper into seams.
        It came back that I had imagined myself
parental sentimental and well-intentioned,
        thinking about a future which may well
        be found false.

I still cannot pronounce the names
        of the students still struggling
with proper nouns, have been pacing the halls
        after class, spending weeknights
working on phonemic script while colleagues
        are reading their kids to sleep.

All of these notebooks and hollow words
        are products of longing: dead things
wanting life, released like bad jokes over empty
        bottles when self-medicating the miles
        she'd call kilometres.

Blame them on those bottles, or on my mother
        asking about the nice girl
in the Florida Facebook photo, or blame them
        on the F.R.I.E.N.D.S marathon that fuelled
a fortnight, or on the pregnant woman
        in the terminal, who asked how I felt
        about "Lauren."

I told her every Lauren I knew was
        lovely; said I wanted a daughter as well,
        some day.

Blame them mostly on me, those non-existent Barker
        daughters whose names were penned
neater than birthday card calligraphy,
        suggesting a care not normally committed to,
        written beside the Chinese characters:
        女孩, 婚姻, 旅行,

        all of my words conflicted.

Homecoming

```
W   T   M   O   E   I       I   T   R   T   T   R
H   O   Y   F   V       T       H   U   H   H   A
E           E   A       E       N   T   E       I   N
N   E   A   M   R   R   I           W   T           F       N
E   N   N   Y   Y   R   S   P           Y   I   F   D
V   G   O       T   I   V   L           M   M       R
E   L   R   R   I   V   E   A           I   M       U
R   A   A   U   M   E   O   N   W               I   M
    N   K   C   E       T   E   H   H   L       M
I   D       K       T   O   T   M   C   O       I
        A   S   I   O   T   M   H   M   A
F   I   T   A       T   H   E   H   E   R
L       C   F   G   E   E               N       G
Y   P   T   K   I   R   T   T   A   S
    A   H       N   E   G   I   E   G   O   A
B   C   E   B   D   Y   R   N   L   A   U   G
A   K       E       R   I   G   A   I   N
C       T   C   T   S   N   G   L   I   D   A
K       O   A   H   K   D       S   N   D   I
        P   U   T   I       H   M   B   O   N
            S   H   E   O   E   E   U   F   S
            E       S   F   T   T
```

ground.

At A Cost

They don't stock Snyder in the bookstores here.
I've been taking walks in the woods on a daily basis
because it's the closest I can come to his pages.

Each morning I spend an extra fifteen seconds showering
which means this time next year I'll be living in the stream,
cleansed – cyclically evaporate/condense... content.

There's a wind farm visible from the bathroom window
but I can only make out the blades above the trees
as they work their way from nine to three repeatedly.

Have long wanted to stand under one and stare upwards,
observe the low swing and feel spotlighted for a second,
only to be routinely forgotten in favour of the clouds.

Alice wrote that those blades fatally interrupt migratory
flights and I've been lying awake most nights, wondering
if Gary would settle for the compromise, clean energy at a cost.

照片

After learning the symbols and the correct
pronunciation I wander back to the new house

repeating the word into the shadow of the
streetlights while flicking through all of the 照片

that have nested like spiders inside my phone
revisiting the night we stole the street signs

or the morning you decided to climb into
the cupboard under the stairs and could not

get out until the early afternoon all stiff and sore
like you'd just run a marathon when you

had actually knotted your limbs in the framework
of the house we made a home and we took 照片

instead of helping you unravel yourself
because we wanted to remember you

at your most unfortunate but ironic and I do
there where you follow two rows of 照片

featuring her Miami and me which you'd said
I should've condemned and a few 照片

of the messages you had sent from San Diego
on your birthday but mostly I found 照片

of nothing of real note just the palm of my hand
or stir-fries in progress perfected for Instagram

and these days I cook for one but make the same
amount and my follower count is down

but my memories are up and I am taking fewer 照片
and thinking about you more often old friend

wondering if I carry you with me when I am smoking
out of the bathroom window and only crushing

on Asian women and writing mostly about dogs
I will never know as well as I knew your own.

Bee Season

Strained   goodbye   outside of
bus   station   in   Baltimore.
Wrote   last   words on stained window,
which she read   backwards as
YSAE TI EKAT   hoping   she got
the   message   Rode   west

bereft   via variety   of   backseats
(half a week) arrived   in   stoned Seattle
weak   &   staggered   to
first   motel met   with
R   MS   AVA   BLE   slept   well
mostly   sleeping   alone

again   Put together   text
expressing   some regret   in   the
shade   couldn't quite   make
out   screen   /   message relayed
wrote   *Wrist you were Gere.*
          Was   surprised

when she   replied   with
picture of   Richard waving   on
set of   *Primal Fear.*   Said   she was
(pretty)   sarcastic   woman
adding   picture from   Lincoln Park
wanting to   ride   luck   little   while
                              longer.

Max Bowden is a poet from London, trying to understand the position technology has taken in our lives. You can find some version of him on twitter @TheOfficialMaxB, and more poems can be found in back issues of *Ink In Thirds* and *The Broke Bohemian*.

earth returns
a poem transmitted from Mortlake Road

full flat beer bottles
speak to ambition
lost in the sunrise
mud dragged in
reads the morning news
laughs at the mess

day blooms / erupts
depending on mindset

the turning of life
appears significant
cars   breaking
cyclists gliding
audible   even
stunning in their volume

pixelated

sometimes i sext in the kitchen
to add flavour to the
meal i'm preparing.

when i am full, unsatisfied,
smoking outside,
i drop and break my phone.

Boxing Day

It's the early hours in my dad's house.
The airbed that never made it
to full is hissing, telling me
about the floor and what it has to offer
my posture   my personality.
Now I am hunched and soft
but the whispering, dying bed
talks of hard times that wait for me.
Rain on the window   taps
the melody of solidity while I think
of all the times I needed toughness,
all the times I folded or swayed
long enough for the world to pass.
I think of your bed and the distances.

The hissing continues, hip to the ground.
I turn, try and lie on my front,
wriggling causing the bed to buck
and seethe – ultimately let down
by this childish behaviour.

My phone lights up the room
letting me know something
happened somewhere else.
I tut and turn it over.
I don't want to know the time.

I had an octopus emoji next to your name in my phone
because I like octopuses and I liked you too.

You were a practised big spoon,
the late night wrap seemed eight arms strong
and I was mesmerised by your intelligence.

I finally changed it when I listened to a podcast
on cephalopods and   fell asleep sad,
thinking about their mythical qualities.

Now   next to your name is a floppy disk
outdated, outmoded, incompatible,
trapped in this poem and the past.

Dustbowl Hellhole

When the Space-Men get to Mars
they'll sell air for 100 starbuks
a day and land prices will skyrocket
due to the presence of an atmosphere.
For these software-simians on Mars
eviction will be existential
hydroponic failures will hit food costs
and showering will become unvogue.
Budget spacelines will cut corners
but they knew what they were buying
when the rocket lights up the sky
and the g-force breaks some ribs.

That capitalist will sit in his dust palace
wanking into piles of red cash
conqueror of Mars, God of stocks,
his next mission to replace people
with AIs all forced to wear his face.

Biology in Action

Thirty desks bearing the marks of
countless deathward glances
where the children settle,
in soil, capsules of life
set to rise and fall within the week.

This impermanence can nurture
a sense of foreboding in young minds
and they take to carving
just like we knew they would.

Soon spreading between young ears,
a way to outlast stuffy afternoons
with no more than a compass,
set toward the varnish,
and a little imagination.

Next to names and insults
or some cave-paint creation,
they set to placing themselves
with more diligence than ever.

selfie selfie groupshot meme

I know you want to be in my life but
is a callous way to break things off
even though we only ever took one selfie
more for the ceremony of first selfie
than any desire to capture a specific moment
I did feel that our moments shared
deserved more than such a cold tone.

I know you want to be in my life but
makes me want to write a poem
about all of your annoying habits
and I did but then   I scrapped it
out of fear of seeming spiteful,
but still I never imagined you
unaware of your words.

I know you want to be in my life but
did sting for a while, won't lie, but
people say worse and it's true I suppose
I did want to be in your life but
that it was mutual was more important
otherwise I'd just follow your Instagram.

ANNA CATHENKA

Anna Cathenka's first pamphlet, *Dead Man Walking*, was published in 2018 by New Fire Tree Press. She holds a first class honours degree in Creative Writing from Falmouth University and was the grateful recipient of the 2017/18 *Ink, Sweat & Tears* scholarship. Links to published reviews and poems can be found at cathenka.wix.com/annacathenka

34

Preface

It is not of course possible to include the whole of the *Anna Cathenka* in a work of this size, but for a long time past it has been the desire of the poet to present to the observant public an introduction to this fascinating field of study.

It happens that the whole of the larger of our *Anna Cathenka*, including those which fly in the day-time and those having the largest and most conspicuous of

      practically the whole of this important group
               large divisions
    has been omitted entirely.

This does not mean that they should be entirely disregarded,

      illustrations are approximately life-size
  (exceptions of eggs)

Since this excellent series is available for the serious student, the author of the present book has omitted details of the adult *Anna Cathenka* and relied on coloured illustrations. The descriptions of the larvae and pupae are short, partly to enable the book to be kept small, and brief field notes have been added.

It is hoped that the result, which can so easily be slipped into the pocket, will provide the observer with an introduction in the field to the study of this compulsive subject.

A Lobster Poem
in duck form

this is the first poem I have written in a long time
that doesn't use primary source material
primarily because Emily & John don't

have any books about lobsters in their house
which is a primarily terrible oversight on their part. usually
the poems I write without primary source material

are terrible which confirms I am primarily
an editor, not a poet. LOBSTERS. also, using someone
else's words takes the pressure off that depth

of feeling that I'm scared of. I like to express myself
in all the things I don't say, am too scared to say
to leave them as blank spaces on the page

here is

          everything

I am afraid of, which you somehow
managed to convey entirely with that look
you gave me. oh fuck. lobsters are not ducks.

lobsters live at tremendous depth. lobsters have
blue blood. lobsters get more fertile as they age. lobsters
taste great. this poem is not about you at all

OK? this is a poem in duck form, it doesn't say
anything it is supposed to. it is a tray. it has conformed
to a three line stanza pattern only

to expose a difficult page break in the middle
which is a clever, postmodern, neo-Olsonic
method of suggesting absence. the words

have left the page! NEPHROPIDAE. lobsters are
invertebrates with a hard, protective exoskeleton. this poem
is not about you. because lobsters live

in murky environments. because lobsters differ from
because lobsters   because when there is
no primary source material to hand then it's just wikipedia

or fear

On Reflection

The ocean is many manoeuvrable things
—Eileen Myles, 'The Guest'

> i want to
> fuck someone
> as big as an ocean
>
> & fall in love
> with them
> because of all
>
> the little critters
> floating in them,
> to be swallowed & obvs
>
> to drown in them.
> you are not even
> a lake, so why ffs
>
> have i fallen in?
> to you i am
> a result
>
> of many manoeuvrable
> things. like dust. an
> aftermath. well
>
> fuck us.
> i might like to be
> a lecturer

one day but
my problem is
i enjoy improving

lives of the people
i fall in love with
only & would really

have to bend the rules
in order to take
any interest

in my students
& would, I guess
get fired.

but I don't know
what else
to do. I can't

mope around after you
you pond
you barely

have any depth
to speak of. i flew
over the kara sea

& there were islands
& ice-floes &
inlets & shit & it was

more exceptional
than every time
you put your dick in me.

but really
i don't want to be
green. i just want

to fuck someone
as serene as siberia
seemed & fall in love

with them because of how
remote they look
as i'm flying

over them. i flew
over you but it was
more like the euphrates,

devastating. i have yet
to find a third
simile for a person

i'd like to fuck
or an abstract
and poetic

reason to fall in love
with them
& just

as
bad things
happen in threes

i cannot relax
until i find that final
simile & will not

fall in love
until i do.
i just know

despite what my cunt
& tongue & teeth &
the chest cavity

that feels
like an imprint of your
horribly perfect

dick/face combo
would have me
believe, it isn't you.

even if
you're so beautiful
it's like your face

was made to mirror
mine &
you make

the space
around yourself
uncanny & I

could've spent
forever, puddle,
reflecting in you

Dark and Deep

The man on the train says *they've
been building this forest for years* and yet
I'm afraid of woodland metaphors
because of Robert Frost. Sorry. It's just

not right to find poetry in everything.
Or is it? Morally, I mean. I worry I might
be a thief or take too much advantage,
am invasive, maybe. You can't magpie

lives like that, especially your own.
They have been building this forest
for years and yet I can only see the trees
and the black hole around which my life

has revolved and which I have to name
so I can start to let go. The man on the train
counts down *THREE* and my heart beats
a little faster *TWO* because I am

going to name it. Not on the train but
here on the page.
                    ONE
                              child abuse.

It is a big forest and seen altogether
the trees almost look real. I can see
how they've paid attention
to the arrangement of species that trees

themselves prefer to adhere to –
the newer parts a lace of silver birch
the older, oaks. Near the river
there is weeping willow by the swathe

and I see beeches are being built up.
They have put in all the right animals
and fungus in all the right places and even
the birdsong is clear. I can see

the forest is as real as I need it to be.
I scan my eye across the canopy
for miles until finally the black hole
appears as a clearing in the mist.

Cai Draper was born in South London in 1988. He recently became godfather to the best human in the world.

Single Form
(after Barbara Hepworth)

The sculpture is of me. A monolith
born of London turf, blue, green, dun gold
teetering. And this curiosity:
its main feature is a perfect circular
space, a lack where metal
was. The words I've flung
through there. Fear, shame,
rage shaped in the rank expression
of language to take flight.
If you know the secret to why we sing
and hide our faces, I am listening.

Nudge

If language flogs the world
into existence   flags us up/down   why then
anxious wind huh?   What's this tidal
spinal fluid?

I reside in revenge   porn   Argos   drones
and credit   These are my elements
ring ring   *What you up to Cai?*
Just chilling

Poetry does very little   & language is barely
a thing at all   *Dad?* I said   as a kid
on the beach   Adults nudged him   *Er yes?*
Just   nothing

Language is a trend   zeitgeist   terrarium   Poetry
is better at night   The only editing I do

Mostly it's all in your head

Extra Terrestrial

                    happy   joyously yes   i video the dead
              kangaroo on my ipad   its feet   lankily protrude
       through its mouth   *damn*   flies rise
                         like birds
                   to flock return to oz

                                                        the
                         out
          back

                   guts on the dust road   'must
                 have   been a truck'   you don't say   scrub
            peels way gumbark to horizon *look!*   the
                 scoffing   we hear   when our
                              guide says
             her people are from the dream time

australia in general   baz luhrmann

    your best bet   maybe mel gibson
              i may leave it there

       ozzie blood   means   i show off a lot
     but i'm scared
                                          of the sea it's too deep   and
              BEWARE OF THE SHARKS   spiders, things
                                           that jump
                 quickly   the main thing
                   i worry about   is not   genocidal racism
                 fatal bugs   or the beach body but
       the way
       the belly   goes
when   my dad and his   partner and   daughter do their

         <MOVING-TOGETHER-AS-A-UNIT>
                         thing
              i'm in the same nation   but   not
on   the same planet

mother's father / dad's dad

i was scared to make this poem /
treat them right / they never
came close to meeting in life
so how to present them dead /
i'd have them here retold as bodiless
friends with shears / with god /
dear holy ghost /
may i bring these families together in death /
can these souls fold up the long haul
between us / here is the pen in my breast
tearing space / the page a sorry place
to compress two lives into one / undie
to feed and sate me now /
these twin forces racing away / i /
a stateless flagpole

Systems

i.

I like my beans from Kenya please
but where's the mud? Waiting in Arrivals
I check bbc.co.uk/food on a tablet for ideas.
I like to buy local with the time of year.
I have even more of a hard-on for James Martin
when he tells me – quote – smoked eel
is a delicious substitute for smoked eel
– unquote – with zero per cent irony.
And the blog says Little Chef's licence
was 'provoked'. I like my eels like I like my people:
physically contained or dead. I wear my favourite
Mexican shirt to the pie and mash shop
and receive bewildered stares.

ii.

Did I say spring came late? The grass
was fake, the birdies went and died
in turbines. They say the bird is on the wing
but that's absurd. They've gone extinct.
I like my seasons like I like my binaries:
increasingly blurred. London, autumn,
Ryanair, spring. Naomi Klein made
a great podcast episode, her laughs
committed and self-effacing.
This was the observation I made
after her: corporations are evil
so portion your meals
and thoroughly sort the recycling.

Blush

nothing says
alive like morning
stench of a downward
glance from a shindig
that went west. nothing heats
the blood like regret. apologies,
disclaimers, confession in sms:
sacred texts. nothing moans here
and now like dawn's wetted
parts. the not knowing
who knows what.

Kat Franceska works as a library assistant and a life model. Her poetry reacts to the everyday and the work of art. She is currently researching the role of the model in art history whilst writing about her experiences of the job.

Waste

It's good for the skin
he said, as he wiped it off my neck.
How can anything leaving a body
be good for you?

When I face the bathroom window,
morning light coming through,
I see hundreds of hairs
on my chest. Not just the thick ones
around the nipples,
I am covered in pale fuzz.
I pluck until I get bored, go red.

A family friend in America
drinks her first wee of the day.
At least I think that's true.

Every period I look in the toilet and
my god, who died?
I imagine all of the children I could have had
but didn't want.
The children I could have
but still don't want.

Aquatics Poem

At the garden centre there were four sections.
COLD WATER full of croaking tetra,
SPECIALIST almost empty,
but it was in MARINE that she saw
a lamarck's angel befriend a plastic jellyfish.
She wanted to note how beautiful it was,
black and white scales brushing up against
neon pink tentacles and bell.

In TROPICAL she witnessed
amano shrimps feasting on a female guppy.
Five piled on the carcass,
their legs scratching,
ripping off white flesh and devouring it.
She wanted to express how upset she was,
as the troupe trailed the tank
sucking up the scraps.

Head Injury

The leaflet says rest and do nothing. Sleep —
don't fight. Lie on the sofa under the fleece blanket.
Listen to music, films or television shows.
Don't concentrate on a screen. No heavy reading.
Rise slowly from bed — this will avoid dizziness.

If you ache, it's okay.
If you are cold, it's temporary.
These states are okay.
Memory loss is temporary.

Sit in quiet rooms. Steer clear of children.
Tell your neighbours to stop arguing, tell their son to stop screaming
and jumping around — there is no need.
Watch snow drip from the roofs opposite.
Hope ice will soon disappear from pavements — you are not steady yet.

If you weep, it's okay.
If you are irritable, it's temporary.
These states are temporary.
Memory loss is okay.

You were in Venice almost exactly a year ago.
Look at your photos, see how focused life could be before.
Put a plaster over the Steri-Strips — don't get the wound wet.
Wear a blue-and-white-spotted shower cap when washing your body.
Seek assistance when washing your hair.

If you feel nauseous, it's temporary.
If you have trouble concentrating, it's okay.
These states are okay.
Memory loss is temporary.

Six Works by Jeff Koons

inflatables made to save a life   to weigh

it down distort reflection   colour it   countless
versions of self   out of laziness
standing horizontal looking at many of you

puts a frame   the tail sits tall
an object so big it fills
every room   remain concerned with self
in the surface   I'm not looking
at it I'm looking in it

a bowl of eggs smooth pink textured white

bouncing pushing through thick
liquid material
there is a wobble

soft   but not

balance heavier solid on heavy solid
make it seem easy   impossible

the ability to indent imprint squish mould push
against press into add to take from make
from malleable   a squashed bear this angle
creases underneath

You'll change your mind when you're older

I am older now was always
old enough to know what I want
wanted didn't want cannot bear to think
of having, I feel a guilt in my gut or perhaps
it's my womb that guilt is not for me he might decide
one day to leave he might want to be a parent I can't help that
can't help with that can't force it can't force my body to carry a future
it won't treasure. What is it to you this choice I've made why is it your business
it has no impact on your life get on with your life ask questions of yourself are you happy
or do you live a certain way because you're expected to are you always this ignorant and rude?
I won't change my mind this is my choice this is my choice I don't get why you think you know better
than I do you are Mystic Meg I am a silly girl you patronise because you're a proper woman who has children and
why wouldn't I want what you have?

Rachel Goodman is a Norfolk native who has taken the scenic route to poetry. Having been variously an actor, mime artist, BBC radio presenter, journalist, portrait painter and mother (she is still the last two), she finally came to rest at UEA, where she was awarded the Bryan Heiser Memorial Scholarship for Poetry.

Nil by Mouth

i am trying very hard to make myself heard
but i have lost my language
languga   lagidj   lagh   glg

i am the fat one the farty one f-foot in mouth clown

throw a slipper and i will fetch it   the furry felt of it
sticks to my tongue   fluff dries my mouth

spit it out then, go on

i am trying very hard to make myself heard

but my words are little woolly balls that roll around the room
you plough straight through   kick them to the walls

you know how tactless you are

you laugh like a broken necklace
beads bounce   everywhere
i caper between your legs   chasing the ping of them

just teasing

pretty shiny things
i suck them up and stuff my cheeks   a horrid hamster
with machine-gun jaws   *pyoo-pyoo-pyoo!*   *ak-ak-ak!*

i want to spray you all with red-hot bullets
but i am not brave enough
to own your burning heads
black tongues crisping out of open mouths

not big enough
to bear the smoking silence of surprise

and so i swallow it   glg

o

I think I know how Alice felt
too big for the room
the ceiling on my shoulders
lips pressed to my knees
all flesh and edge
and breathless o

I don't want these
arms ears cheeks
breasts thighs lungs tongue
squeezed
by four walls and a floor
I'm greedy for shrinkage

drink me

I'll swallow it
the label says I can
but o will I just be
squared smaller

      painted   blue
      s c i s s o r e d
      made   to   fit?

it's not a question of scale
but of dot-ness
if I am just mouth o
you'll have to hear me.

In the days when TV programmes were all done by twelve
the black and white screen closed down its brightness,
starting at the sides and fading to a dot. I watched it
once, long after bedtime   disappearing.

I couldn't take my eyes of it.

o   I said   o

drink me

it might be poison
but I'll risk it
for the sake of dot-
ness

Personal Quarters

My first real home
under four kitchen chairs
had pink candlewick walls
detufted, a trail of bright dots
where the fluff had rooted once
        I Listened with Mother
        but she was always washing up
        with a migraine and a string of pearls.
Every two years we were posted to a different patch,
marched out by quartermasters
with their clipboards listing army issue items
one silver cruet, plated, officers for the use of.
        Mother said moving was such a headache
        but she had it down to a T
        and always packed the teapot last.
The curtains and the carpets stayed behind,
we took black Baa Lamb and the gramophone,
a silver cigarette box, Sgt Pepper and Monopoly.
There was always a new school,
        when she did my plaits her hands smelled
        of Atrixo and the inside of her rubber gloves.
        Hair snagged in the sapphires.
We took it in turns to choose bedrooms
but every house had the same darkened place
we tiptoed past each month being good girls.
        Mother told me
        once the pain was so bad
        she banged her head
        against the wall hard
        really hard
        on purpose
        trying to bash it out of her
        had she drawn blood
        spattered the magnolia?

        a trail of bright dots

Ride a White Swan
School sanatorium: temperature 102°

i have no mother
my sheets have been pulled
by a Sister wearing lipstick
i heard her
white nylon coat rasping
someone
will look in on me later
someone   *da-da-di-di-da*
time has dried
to the far thump of girls' feet on floorboards
        and i am as lonely as i have ever been
they are in the blue hour before bed
bitching beneath Marc Bolan
        and i am as lonely as i have ever been
my landscape is lunar and quiet
seven white beds lie with me
whisper it
someone   *da-da-di-di-da*
        my throat is not mine
        the strangest thing is me
straight in my sheets
i want a white breast to lean against warm
feathered
write me a sick-note Marc
cry your black tears from the classroom wall
Miss Brooke will understand
but leave me a page
ragged along its edge
which might tell me where my rage was born
whisper it Sister   *da-da-di-di-da*
no one
could say i went unattended

Orange Rachel

a ping-pong ball thrown into a bowl in 1966   plop
won me a goldfish at the village fete
won me a goldfish   and some water   but not the bowl
I took it home in a plastic bag
they said I could keep it in my bedroom   if
I fed it and looked after it   they said
it was up to me to keep it alive
I named it Orange Rachel
and spent two weeks' pocket money on a bowl
and some fish food   I think she liked it
she went round and round and grew fat
I tipped out a handful of flakes   every day

     [I hadn't yet taken the lid off kindness or neglect]

and watched her swimming   round and round
my eyes refracted huge and globular
until I forgot   to feed her
and she was taken to Rosabelle's pond
decanted
and lived a happy life they told me
until a heron got her   oh dear   I didn't cry

     [that was the death of Orange Rachel]

over the years
other things came into my hands to be cared for
things I named   things I could keep   if
I fed them and looked after them
I kept on throwing ping-pong balls   1977   /88   /99
some bounced across open mouths
some landed   plop   and I got to take them home
all my Orange Rachels   I didn't forget

     [it was up to me to keep them alive]

I tipped out a handful of flakes every day
careful to keep the balance between kindness and neglect
not wanting to overdo it
nor deny them what they needed
they seemed to like it   they went round and round
and grew fat

then one day   when I am gazing
my eyes refracted huge and globular
I open my palm and ask   *is this the right amount?*

you say

you shouldn't have said that – it isn't appropriate
I'm shocked – don't cry: this isn't about you –
this is about me taking responsibility for my anger

and with one huff you blow the flakes away and leave me
empty-handed   now
should I close my fingers to a fist and punch you in the mouth
or dip again into the tin   and bring out more

        [is it up to me to keep it alive?]

Laurence Hardy taught English in Europe and Asia. Before coming to UEA, he studied under Cliff Forshaw at Hull University. He plays guitar.

My Old Address Book

reads like a bestiary.
A late twentieth-century rarity
full of exotic species
now dead or endangered.

Some notable entries include:
a minotaur stuck in a maze of honey.
There's a sphynx, a squinting lynx,
a matador stroke playboy bunny.
There's a liger, medusa,
a vermillion bird of the south.
There's a dodo, a calma,
patasola, a piguana.

But for all that wonderfauna
my drawings fall short.
One dimensional.
Badly observed.
Like a poor man's
Villard de Honnecourt.

Sonnet For Self Assembly

One witness likened the cloudring that formed

Above the A-B Bomb to a pool of spilt milk.

In old photos shot from high windows

The street is a board game the pieces people.

In my poems bureaucrats can hurt me more

Than the circumference of an atom split.

NASA's space paparazzi shoots and stores

Long shadows of satyrs and eunuchs.

Meanwhile I drown in my de-composition

Can't think with fingers like puppeteers

Or see through corners like rally drivers

I want to but no has the remote control.

Before they cut me open, count the rings

Put a stethoscope here and listen.

Before I Teach You How To Play Guitar

Feed it bar chords
Greensleeves, Sweet Georgia Brown
Licks, harmonics
Arpeggi, pentatonics
Burn out Blind Blake's
Ragtime thumbs
Mississippi John's
Breezy mixolydians
Watch as Segovia,
Rodrigo disappear
Narciso's twelve strings
Couldn't save him
As a sprig of heather
Won't save a gypsy
From the phrygian
Flamenco spiral
Descent into O.

Lorca likened the guitar to a tarantula
That spins a star to suck in lost sighs
Johnson didn't deal with the devil
The delta bluesman sold his soul to Einstein.
Don't expect Mr Crowley to un-hex you
Once you're in the pull of the pupil
In the shadowed canthi of its Nefertiti eye
The helter-skelter spell of anti-matter spells
            GAME OVER.
The darkest energy known to musos
Blacker than the blackest of black holes
From this moment on, you're its apostrophe
Because soundholes are the true singularities...

Now let's begin with an open E.

there is a ˡʷᵃʸˢ/gap — there is a^{lways}_{gap}

be^{tween}_{hind} the l^{ight}_{oo roll} hitting the re^{tina}_{ctum}

and the s^{ight}_{mell} that f^{orms in}_{reezes} the mind

same must hold true for what I t^{ouch}_{aste} and h^{ear}_{ere}

so, I a^{ssume}_{t first bite} , that p^{lums taste like peaches and}_{eaches taste like plums}

at least for that ^{micr}nan_{pic}o-sec those s^{ignals}_{ensations}

race round the tight canals of the fleshy stone

and what about melons vs lemons

as the brain compares the s^{weetness}_{ourness}

against all the s^{weetnesses}_{ournesses} it has ever previously k^{nown}_{icked}

is there a ^{micr}nan_{pic}o-mo when s^{weet}_{our} are same

do the t^{ickle}_{orture} of s^{oft fur}_{andpaper} on the skin

begin life not yet s^{plit}_{awn apart}

in the g^{rey}_{lassy} mire of the m^{ind}_{irror of the}

m^{ind}_{irror of the}

m^{ind}_{irror of the}

(some notes on Subatomic Poetry)

This poem was written under strict l^{aboratory}/_{aborious} conditions
ooney tune

P^{oems}/_{oets} only have t^{endencies}/_{ic(k)s} to ex^{ist}/_{pel}

Think of it like t^{his}/_{ank-pong}

This poem starts p^{ossibly here}/_{robably here}

It is i^{mportant}/_{nsane} to r^{ealise}/_{ead quietly on} the l^{aws}/_{oos} of sub^{atomic}/_{buteo} poetry

However, no^{one}/_{t even Niels Bohr} can say for sure w^{hat a}/_{ord} will b^e/_{ingo}

Do not r^{ide}/_{ub} a poem in search of a poet

Subatomic poets are un^{stable}/_{gover}
der no circumstances ^{to be approached}/_{to be left alone}
with^{out supervision}/_{in flammable buildings}

They will, th^{ough}/_{ankfully} , sooner or later, fall into d^{ecay}/_{isco overdrive}

When they start to dis^{integrate}/_{co-combobulate} , stand well back

At this point they are un^{stable}/_{gover}
der no circumstances ^{etc}/_{etc}

Strap on you g^{oggles}/_{onads} if you got 'em

Now see the unity of all things

The visual model of this poem looks like a b^{ra}/_{one}
alalaika

the aling of muse on
harmony achine

ink clap, solar yin
tel, tr lun ang

or will the occasional provide the perfect
aident de

I am the people in when I say
erson

in theory material in
e nuclear matter e

could be to the size of a full stop
ompressed top.

That's not, far from it
to say an inert d

protons back and forth at 40,000 miles
ace second

his
minus that locosmic dot

nergy
the rest of me is electron playground

I am my bodyweight in
OOMS

no wonder wear such colourful jumpers
ew agers ling to trees

better love trees than the tall glass sanctions of the city. Stop

Iona May is a poet from Bristol, where she was also a secondary school teacher. Her mother's death has become a central motif in her writing this year. Drawing on her clown training, Iona's poetry takes the trivial seriously and shows the ordinariness in catastrophe.

Get Well Soon Cards sold at the hospice

Can love congeal
into words on card?

Who is this incantation protecting?

that draws you to this deathbed   my mum's

last light burning brighter

you are moths   kethwump! kethwump!   please stop   please

observe the timetable it took me so long to figure it all out   do you want me to cry   let me

comfort you   death is so ubiquitous or She stopped being

fat or we die every second according to buddhism or we all live forever according to everyone or She's

my mother so maybe   She'll start screaming and the nurses won't listen

when i tell them to force feed the oxycodone so   please go She's wasted

the morning flirting with doctors *you have to*   they keep you alive and now She can't talk

please stay i don't know   *what to do if She stops*

Iona are you too scared to let anyone love you? I was but I'm over it I don't need your help

to walk I'm as solid as a rock trust me we could make an escape

my friends don't mention death because it's impolite   unbearably lonely

we say   a life lived with the strength of a warm heart   please it's not true
that's what you'd say about a dead person   *I want to be buried in my pyjamas*
so it's cosy   it was so nice but
                    i spoke to Her on the phone

i was pretending   i can feel Her presence too or i think
dad's doing ok or please ask about me   i hate that or i'm fine or what a relief or She was lucky
to die young   so all Her friends could attend   to Her beck and call

no you can't visit today we are all too weary and I know that means you probably won't see Her again

I understood the contours of your shoulders they were so brave they wanted to fold inwards to protect the soft place at your centre because there is too much clamorous light out there for a body that is losing her mother in a classroom where teenagers are so disgustingly alive with the jabber of their insecure edges your

shoulders were iron enough like armour not fragile like wings but scared of appearing too small with bad posture in a classroom where you thought they should be intimidating I was there with my shoulder-pads and together we opened but did not expose because I gently hugged the ache of you and was red for *keep out danger*

of death in a classroom where red can't be sexy I was loose to make your breasts unimportant but could feel them within me close then receding with your ribcage with your lungs with the need for air and your heart *still here still here still here* and the pace of it was the panic of you until we steadied then this was a classroom

where we conducted their insights and the way your arms moved was so exhilarating but we don't do that anymore you don't need me like you used to

Watching the dancers

I want to be able to fly more than anything but
if I needed to work for it by doing things like jogging in the morning and
moisturising nightly would I bother? I can jump. In the moment before falling there's
all the people I don't see every day anymore and how little we touched and how often we
said how are you?　　　　My waist is still so available.　Anyone
could just rest their hand here and

Abstract

Although most children have high creativity levels ($L_{10} - L_{12}$), approximately 98% of adults in the United Kingdom have critically low creativity ($L_1 - L_5$) (Dawlish & Blande, 2014). Our previous study showed a positive correlation between the retention of creativity levels of secondary school students and their teachers' creativity levels (Livingstone & May, 2012). Additionally, it has been well documented that hares naturally retain L_{12} creativity due to their photosynthesis of moonbeams. Due to the lack of homo sapien adults with the creativity levels required to reverse the dullness pandemic, there is a need for an intervention to ensure that children retain their creativity levels through adolescence. For this purpose, the current study SapienMorphed six hares into homo sapiens. The SapienMorphed hares (femina sapiens) were randomly assigned to six secondary schools across East Anglia for a period of four years. The study then tracked the creativity levels of the students taught by the femina sapiens and compared them to the creativity levels of students taught by homo sapiens. It was hypothesised that the students taught by femina sapiens would have higher creativity levels than that of the control group; however, the results are inconclusive. We recommend further enquiry into femina sapien assimilation of effective teaching methods.

Keywords: dullness pandemic, SapienMorph, femina sapien, creativity levels, moonbeams

The Femina Sapien

When I slept on the earth I knew everything but I'm losing it all in the echo of my shoes in here. When I step there's a ceiling below me and where is the sky?

I arrange the students in squares because that's what you do in here. The students make stench of their hopes that ricochet and what do they want? My ghost ears flatten.

Black tights itch but if my legs kicked out of them I'm sure I would vanish. I've never felt sweat like this. Never noticed my eyes are looking out my face. Never looked frontwards.

The earth used to throb through my body. I was movement and knew all the moving of earth things. Grasses do not whisper and what did they say? I'm losing it all in the squares.

In here their limbs and their voices still ricochet. I point at the title with my fingers *okay quiet. Three. Two. One. Write the date and the title.* How else could I make all their hopes fit?

My ghost ears lift high but what should I say? The scientists told me the Socratic method is moonbeams. I call out to all those hopes in those squares *listen, you will be so Socratic.*

It seems you want everything but where is the sky? They say *miss, we already know there is no God.* There is though that feeling of dusk. I'm losing it all in the language of my shoes in here.

There actually were not any Get Well Soon Cards sold at the hospice. They did sell cards but with things like just flowers on them. There was a café in the foyer and I sometimes sat there and that is where they sold the cards. I cannot remember why I sat there. It is odd because, surely, I would have gone home if I was not in her room. They sold cake and I sometimes bought some. It was disappointing cake but that was fine. I thought how funny it would be if they sold Get Well Soon Cards. I glanced at the cards to check but I could not see anything saying Get Well Soon. Maybe I sat there because people wanted to have time alone with her or maybe I did not have the energy to cycle home yet. It was such a long cycle and such a hot summer.

I think I collect anecdotes like the one about the Get Well Soon Cards because it is something to say. Another anecdote is that my sister once said that we can measure how bad things are getting by the number of cards we receive. That is true, especially in that I found it hard to notice Mum's deteriorating health. It also shows that my sister used poetic anecdotes too, so it is not just me. We did get a lot of cards. The messages in them were lovely and I sometimes judged people on their poetic skills or tried to work out their subtext. Other times I felt touched. Often, I did not read them properly.

I had planned a walking holiday in Turkey and bought a map and a guide book but then all the cards arrived so I realised I should cancel my plans. That is not true. I did make those plans but I cannot remember whether or not my cancelling them correlated with the influx of cards. It must have been about a month before she died, she must have been obviously extremely ill, but I spread the map over the sitting room floor and hunched over it to plot my route with a pencil.

Keeley Middleton writes about the frustration of using language to express, living with mental health, existential ache, heartbreak and growing up. She performed in the renowned Cambridge University Festival of Ideas, headlined CB1 and has been published in *Mint*, *Paper Plane Pilots* and *Crisp*. Follow her on constantasanorthernstarx.wordpress.com

Eggs

i / truth / eggs / i beauty them when they shimmy / in the pan and goad
me into grating cheese / i cannot make an omelette the way gran did
when her hands didn't shake / so / you need salt and pepper with eggs
/ an egg without salt and pepper is like a hug without love / eggs are
runny in the pan but if you beat them they take more shape / mum
always makes me an omelette when i come home and reminds me of the
definition of home / fullness / i am full / because i cannot leave / food
on my plate and the omelette is full / it's a beauty / sight to be holding
/ gently like contact lenses or snow globes / in the nursing home gran
cannot make / an omelette / at home / mum doesn't want to make /
them anymore because she is sick of hearing the crack / i swallow them
whole / shell and all / truth / full / i do this / the first time / we kissed /
i said you were un-cracked like an egg / an egg
                              / eggs

Space Movies

                    -- I am the child left
              behind while you time travelled.
         For you it may have been five minutes,
          for me it was years. Not even sure you
                      came back --

         -- I've travelled through wormholes
      met a photocopy of you on a beach I've seen
               ghostlings, frantic book
              shelves, a needle in the sky.
                No-one else knew you
                     were gone --

Hi this is that feeling you forgot
about you didn't text back so
I'm just checking in on you
honey do you have enough
fruit? Are you there God it's
me, masturbating in italics
and somehow crying at the
same time, can we serve
ice cream in bowls tonight
I've gotten tired of the same
old crunchy cone, I've had
the same favourite flavour
for 15 years but at one point
you have to wonder
is it just because I keep saying
it is, everyone says mint
choc chip is their favourite
what a load of bullshit you can't
have the same favourite flavour
unless you're me so here's a subtle
marketing strategy for rum'n'raisin
raisin hopes raisin dreams raisin
minimum wages in the frozen dairy
industry, I do like pistachio but not
like I like you R'N'M, I like you have liked
you for 15 years. Dear Quentin Tarantino
get away from my sister's feet, tell your
boy John Travolta we've heard the stories
about him following people late at
night at the gym and while we're at it
Tarantino I liked that time in that
film that wasn't yours that you fell
down the subway stairs it made
me laugh and I like to laugh that way
when you spurt anything
you're eating or drinking out of
your mouth or nose
trust me the worst one
to have is milk out of your nose
it stings like an allergy, in a way

I can't keep down any substance
that would nourish me
quod me nutrit, me destruit -- that's latin
for *Hello MTV welcome to my*
crib it's full of rotting unchildren
what's the word for not wanting to die
wrong; the way Amy Winehouse did when in
recovery, face first, having choked
on her vomit as the papers printed
pre-written puns about her name
and celebrity cold cases chalked her life
down to being oh so unfortunately
bipolar? Dear childhood home that
my family still lives in, stop letting mould
grow on the walls; Dear squishy
walls, take ownership of the microbes; let's go
back; Dear Moonbeam that touches my
face when I finish work late, how
does it look when I read old messages from people
that don't love me anymore? Dear romantic
poetic tradition, why didn't you send me a letter
back? I'm so scared to try new ice cream
flavours, find something that tastes
amazing and have to replace you rum'n'raisin,
I'm telling you now all these love poems
are about you, milky milky goodness anyone that tells you
any different is a liar or lactose intolerant or
an academic who thinks they know what the writer
was thinking the punchline is I'm not thinking
anything I'm plagiarising my heart
that putrid heart that clichéd fart ventricle
that one that gave love a sad name, that pulsing
whinnying muscle full of tar and ache that one
day will become angina and then will stop.
And then what, then what, whattety what
what are we doing here, at the end of
this line, at the end of
this thought, at the end of
still longing, still writing
sweet everythings in the blue nowhere

Afterparty

who am i to write this when it has been in your mouth / between the
teeth / behind the fillings / shiny and foreign / the teeth / they would
shawshank the hell out of there if they could / i can't leave the line like
that / go back / i want to say please but i don't want to write it down in
case you throw it back at a later date / please throw it / gone off milk
/ go back to the teeth / your mouth / it makes me gag the way you do
when you sneeze / your mouth mainly snot / wishfully doublethink it's
spit / but you know the truth / you read the wikipedia / let's be honest
/ snot dripping down your throat gives you flashbacks to that time
you dropped mbone and it fell down the back of your throat / hourly
intervals / you couldn't get the image of a petrol nozzle dripping onto
concrete out of your head / i write your poems again so i can try to know
you better / when will the moon have the affair / the moon glows in a
way you don't see well but you remember / i know they were the glory
days / knowing isn't in the name it's in the glottal stops / i saw how
our language took root in one another / there's a medical name for
that extraction / my dentist said it would hurt and provided a lollipop /
when was the last time that we looked at other / like we weren't burning
buildings / looking for exits / that don't exist / don't read the next line
/ don't read the next line / don't read the next line / go back to the
beginning / this is where I keep you

Bug

wanna live again like it's 1999 wanna go back to before
when my mum let slip my dad still earns £9.50 an hour
wanna stop adding up how many small successes in life i
would have to make happen so he could retire
        i don't even like him anyway   don't
wanna pretend i've got it bad that it people use as a
euphemism for a crush or hereditary disease you got it
so so bad.
in 1999 everyone tried writing on paper everything on
the computers before good old y2k bug took em out
wrote word for word their 75 thou sci-fi novels about a
3 breasted ninja princess and warlocks, whose life was
very similar thematically to buffy the vampire slayer but
for anticipating copyright difficulties definitely wasn't
i've got it bad, kid whatever it is take your laptop to the
repair shop to get it defragmented because there's a file
somewhere corrupted in 1999 i was a paying member of
the barney the dinosaur fan club you can see pictures
of me in the hat box repurposed for carbon dated carbon
copies of this caligula descent into madness look i'll
show you there's this one picture where i'm sat next to all
of my barney videos and there's another one where i'm
tabbing the ocean thinking there's a god watching me
and ready to wreak revenge well come and get me bug
come and
get me

Bec recently found out that she was a poet, and is still figuring out how to be one. She came to the University of East Anglia expecting to leave with a BA in English Literature, but she discovered a love for the stuff and so enrolled on the Poetry MA.

untitled

it felt like enough to hang myself upside
down by the backs of my knees
on the top bar of a goal post
for the redrush to ring slowly
downwards or upwards
stinging whichever way it would to my temples
and i as red faced girl
could watch upside down football on astroturf skies
but now I have to fill my boots with sand and lead
and walk to the middle of the ocean

and i as red seaweed head girl
am pressed hard by all the blue of it
stood solitary in the expanse
suspended by it all i can root myself
by curling my toes upwards
in untied boots two sizes too big
and down here there is almost nothing
but sand and heavy blue pressing
swill ringing into my ears and
so much solid blue broken only by
my red algae bloom of hair
and the coiling fronds of untied laces
in my peripheral

i wait on the sea bed
swaying in undercurrent timings
to meet with the swell of some manic shoal
black bellied with silver heads
making themselves one iridescent pulsation
they carve a roughly me shaped hole in it
as if my skin has three hundred more layers down here
and around i as wild red haired girl they silver and flicker
silvering and flickering
bodies or body shifting and darting
eyes dartingly shift
to me or to each other inside beating gilled faces

but all at once they dip
what was blue now
is some type of pink
now on clouds the shoal blacken themselves out
into a wing beating flock writhing in black feathers
they open beaks to squawk mad poetry at me
as they dipdance on the pink
underbelly of a football pitch sky

i throw down or up my arms in the thick of it
and the fish are back dancing in light
in silver again and blue again and they dart away
from me into the dense mist of it and i am the closest
i'll ever get to not existing or existing down here
the press of it makes me heavy or nothing
completely here now or now not at all

i see a new spectacle in the distant blue
she hasn't come close like the shoal do
but she is big or massive or a better word for it so
i can watch her fat grooved belly
dipdive in or out of the thick of it
in and out of focus so i think to squint
now i see her barnacled mouth clutching
at the white tatter remains of her dead calf
she hums the water in baritone around us all
floods my ears with this wail so solemn now
heavy it beats in my ear as it swells the sea up thick

but low moan turns to tinny whistle blow
a lighter sound now ringing through the easy pink of it
half time or full time on the astroturf sky
silly helium referee waving her arms at me
helium baby bouncing down off a mother's knee
her arms are waving still and i think
she wants me *down off of that post girl*
helium baby's tattered white blankie
floats up fallingly to the plastic sky
but i pinch my eyes shut up there
and pretending my arms are blanket wings
fold them across the torso of me
so that i might just seem
to be sleeping like a bat

salt stings of the wet blue
prickle at my eyes widened by
the new closeness of you
dragged dead calf you
your skin softened and peeling off you
hanging limp from her labouring mouth
you look sodden through somehow
your ripple skin an extreme of the pruning
grooves now disfiguring the tip of my index finger
that points itself instinctively at you
as if to show my mum here
with a snorkel clamped between her lips
witnessing you as i have done
but she isn't invited to this sea bed
she wouldn't like the empty of it
or we wouldn't want to scare her with
i as underwater girl
you as ghost calf
i as seaweed-woman girl
you as white tatter calf
i as fat-bellied-whale-mother grieving girl
you as soft tendril ghost
i as what are you for now girl
i as

what are you doing up there girl
shrill voice of helium referee
unamused by the i as bat girl routine
dreading when i as the-right-way-up girl
make my dizzy headed landing
i'm about to slink down now but redrush
hits my head hard and takes me clean with it

i watch a jellyfish dream
a pulsating wild body of a thing
so red and pink and string against the blue of it
looks like a soggy mass of ripped tissues
thrown into the sea bloody having
been stuffed into knickers as a makeshift sanitary pad
i dreamt this jellyfish before but
as a red gelatinous mass that had spilled
or spewed out of the leg holes of my knickers
pulsating itself out of me while i slept stinging
or burning its red tentacle trails into my pink thigh flesh
i wake forceful from the placebo pain of it

but on a bed of prickle plastic green now
not on a dream on a white or reddened bed no
just helium referee letting it sigh out of her blowhole
facing down at me with the tassels of
a sleek ponytail slopping over the sides
of her head that is shaking itself at my episode
i as *you're always causing a scene* girl
as *stand up now will you* girl
as *you need to ground yourself* girl

and my eyes are back in the blue thick
and my eyes are beginning to roll to whites now
and my lungs are filling with the thick now
so my wrinkle skin soles
arch instinctively and
my feet slip out
of the untied boots
my face finds the sun
arms and legs press together
and i as dead sardine girl
as red and flesh girl
float dartingly
to the surface
toes pointed
eyes open
streaming
through
blue

Ellen Renton was born and grew up in Edinburgh, before moving to Glasgow to study for an undergraduate degree in English Literature. Scottish identity and culture form the basis for much of her writing, as does her experience of visual impairment. She enjoys experimenting with sound and performance in poetry.

contact

     drawn folds show blotched dawn
         yawns
     roll on robes of smoke
     thoughts fog-soaked   raw
         hold on
     crawl to Os of hope
     to know more   compose
         don't drop   those globes won't
     thaw what floats throatlocked
     all floor-torn
                  oh
         not on nose
     own goal
         slow
         not launched or thrown
               so close
         soft   go on
     left – done
     one down one to go
     please lend me the world whole
     not kept under dust for someone else
         ugh, nearly
     too early
     to beg for body to work yet   each bone
     sleep poached
         forget the rush, don't
         leap or rub just
         gentle touch
               yesssss
     contact

     I win a staring match
     against the day that woke me speechless
     somehow, smaller now

     and in defeat he hands my tongue back
     as if to say he was only
     keeping the words warm while I slept

Hoojicapiv
/huːdʒɪkaːpɪv/

Grandad has a word that carries all the lost ones

    Can you pass the hoojicapiv?[1]
    I'll get you a hoojicapiv[2]

I assumed you knew what I meant
when I said that London had kept its lid on

    This sky is only as impossible
    as the cousin I'll never be taller than

    I find a quiet safety in clouds that
    tuck me in

    I always bloat my hoojicapiv[3]
    with too much milk

    Did you ever soak toilet roll and
    fling it at bathroom ceilings?

    There's a hoojicapiv[4] in all
    the footsteps

    Hoojicapiv[5]

    I stood on hoojicapiv[6] on a
    hoojicapiv[7] and said something
    similar. No one understood me
    then either

1 TV remote
2 Tissue
3 Cereal
4 Stillness
5 Everything feels pregnant
6 Portobello Beach
7 Christmas Eve

the accident will happen
soon enough that we just
taste his prime before
it sours

bad news will be tar
in the camera   the sound will
go funny   under
water   the walls will
be white

the accident will only
be spoken of under
cloak of cough

he will get angry
once   they will be
at home   wife will
dustpan and brush the
chaos then cradle
his head   childlike

he will not be too
handsome because this
could happen to anyone
the actor will be trained
disabled

there will be no paper
work and no physical
pain this is a powerful and
uplifting story about what
it truly means to be human

there will be nice people
who offer sessions with
chairs in a circle   he will
try to crumple the leaflet
he doesn't need their advert
teeth or new approaches

friends won't have
time to learn him all
over again they have
lives and kids and
holidays to take

wife will stay lipsticked
and loyal   she will only cry
alone   and not
for the neighbours

they will spend a Sunday
with his parents who have high
standards and a new linen
tablecloth   later mum will
apologise for letting her
temper fizz over

he will never play the card

it will be too much to ask
to ask for things so he
will not and he will not
talk about the asking

there will be words like
miracle and special and
hope

there will be a close up   his
throat will pulse with the
sinking weight of pride as he
unfolds his feelings for
the nice people   he will feel
better

he will cross the line or solve
the problem or kiss the
trophy and shake the hands
of the friends who were too
busy because life is short

be badged an inspiration
because doesn't it make
you
      awwww

he will learn human
truths about what it
truly means to be
human   he will donate
his old suits

the nice people will be
there   they will know
themselves as the true
heroes   they saw the
human in his foreign
body but they will let
him have today

make you remember
what the world made
you forget   what it
truly means

there will be
a key change

when people stare
he will ask wife why she
stays and she will say that
she loved him before
this   hideousness and
tsunamis couldn't stop her

he will realise that life
had got in the way of all
of the living of it   will
discover a beauty in the
rain will stop wearing a
watch will stop saying
no

he will succeed despite

Derby Day Morning

I've even surprised myself by how quickly I've dropped
the habits   we need to be on that train by eleven   this
is a city of two halves and at the end of the day one
of them will   be guttersludge under the other's shoe   shouldnae
have worn this blue   if anyone asks, just say Partick
Thistle   this city'll no make space or spare you   that should
be early enough to get out before kick off   a few months
somewhere else and already my grip on weekends like this
is loose   they make sure it's earlier in the day now, less time tae
sink pints   I'd think twice   and there's nae going oot
tonight d'ye hear me?   maybe even earlier, the subway will
be a nightmare   ah tell ye it's the clean-up that must cost
them   all that glass vodka-lobbed   all the traffic's
stopped   ah mind a few years back someone bitter threw a rock
tae give oor windae a bailiff shake   or maybe we could
wait til after the whistle   bit risky, probably better just to
go before   the trains chuck them up to take lumps over high
schools and surnames   different words their great
grandads sang tae praise the same god   it's our own fault
we forgot   I can already hear the first chords   they shouldn't
be singing that   that Sectarian Act, ah thought there were
rules now?   cover yer wee ears up darlin   ah know ah can't
stop ye son, ah'm just sayin keep yer heid down   I don't
like the way those songs we shouldn't know sound

Westmost Close

we blew the name of the street through our teeth
        wwwessstmos—
           discovered it's hard to get your lipsa
           round the last bit unless you let
           go of the *ts* and string everything else
           into one wwwhhesssmosclos

we agreed this was a funny name but couldn't decide why:
           maybe because it moved through
           the mouth like the gulls that hooped
           our heads soon to come
           scudding down for crumbs

           maybe because somewhere
           on our descent to daft
           we had renamed it kanyewwwhhesssmosclos

           the sides of my speech turned liquid
           at the thought of him
           keeking over the harbour wall
           to see how clear it was across to Fife,
           a box fresh left Yeezy now puddledrunk

           or maybe it was knowing that this
           was once the edge of things
           before they built the gym, the ASDA, the affordable flats
           the most west that Leith could stretch

Jessica O'Brien Rhodes is a writer and poet. Her work can be found in *Alien Mouth*, *Be About It*, *Leste*, two UEA undergraduate anthologies, and Salò Press anthologies *Milk* and *An Obscurity of Poets*.

Succinct & original pool. A landfill of deflated beloved plastic pools. Ophelia in her last pool. Friday night disco of floating pubescent sexuality pool. Multi-century child ankles pool in the park. Forgotten outdoor state school pool of rain & algal photosynthesis. 630B C in Lesbos pool where in up to the thighs you call me Anna Karenina & say nothing else. The shared pool of childhood screaming & a solid shit's soft eternal sink. Pool so unmeasurably deep a dithering blue. Pool of salt my mother & her mother floating under the sun in bathing suits & me naked in a tank in Vauxhall together somewhere our cuts stinging ecstatically. Pool of imma terial space & language that I like to keep open on my screen & look @ you from across.

Would you rather have unlimited space travel
or unlimited sea travel?

He tells me *it's space*
I would rather die than move to the moon
I have thought about not
having a baby there
is so much healing to do
starting with me
there are so many lakes
and woods to litter pick starting with
me and someone dropped a crisp packet

someone dropped a crisp packet

I would probably forget this planet after
a year if the moon was clean leaving my home
planet all the gravity
all the loss
of it might ruin my posture which is a thing
people can use to read whether you hate yourself or not I can't
be the mum that the other mums think *hates herself*
not on the playground no
not on the moon
and people have left
shit everywhere on the moon it reminds me
that I have only used a hand mirror
to look at my vagina twice
and he says *yeah*
The Blue Planet is cool and technically
plastic didn't kill the baby whale.

*

In one of the matriarchal versions of earth there was a race to get to the
bottom of the sea They sent dogs first The term *seadog* has a different
and melancholic resonance there

In one matriarchal version there was no race is no concept of
competition They have no space travel no knowledge of space beyond
astronomy and entire tabloids of astrology and know the sea intimately
more than we will

I can go o
n

After all is said and done I can still feel so special and rare

In my puffer jacket I am a big red pedestrian
a toddler in a photograph developed from film
a Britney in the *Oops!...I Did It Again* music video
a James Dean in the film *Rebel Without a Cause*

I am in the latest trend one hundred
thousand girls are in red puffer jackets this month
alone

Is this the first time you've said *I'm gonna come* with lips
wrapped around the tip of your cock I want to know
the full names of all the girls you've ever said it to
so I can find them on Facebook I want to throw
a party where we all wear red puffer jackets and
caption the selfies with Morrissey lyrics and *Lolita* I want us all
to walk to Tarzana and shave our heads in Esther's Haircutting Studio
on Thursday
16.02.2017

Exercises

Starting in the tips of your toes move your body one piece at a time until
you reach the forehead

I did not say do it sexily he said

I was moving in a way
I was moving my hips
I was moving in a way before I knew what it did
I was moving in a way before I knew it did
I was moving in a way
I was moving in a way I knew what it would do I didn't know what it did
I was moving in a way I knew in a way what it would do
I was moving in a way and it did and I knew in a way
I was moving in a way I knew
I was in a way moving in a way I knew
I was moving in a way
I was moving my hips
I was moving my hips

*

Follow your finger with your eyes. Fixate at the finger suspended in the
air on the end of your arm. Move your eyes to this position before the
finger is there

It can be more intimate when you look the other way
and the finger moves through the air
as you bend your neck in
the direction of another place

*

At dusk in a large empty field find the moon. Go to the farthest point
from it and then walk slowly towards it not breaking your stare.

This is what it could feel like to walk to the moon.

As you stare imagine your body rising closer like you and it are only
two satellites swimming
in worming light
several pale amoebas
in blue blue blu

When you begin to reach the opposite end
come back slowly

Blue moon, 31.01.2018 – a weekend of a poem

orange peel on the street
the peel of some oranges
the peel of a fruit, some things
un real

but three grey-haired women walking back from the yoga class
three grey-haired women with yoga mats on their right shoulders

leashed foetus you are just an imagination game and I still
sit in the back room of the pharmacy talking over my options
leashed foetus maybe one day I will write you real and I still
won't

I cross to the sunny side of the street
and cross back to the shade

two small plastic spoons, one white and one purple with daffodil
sprouts around
the surface above the root of a tree, a small boy
on a wooden vehicle on a piece of string being towed by a woman
chatting to a woman
down the street, whipped cream laughing-gas canisters

and I am overjoyed for more or less
      a part

*

orbit around me orbit –
how to be a cathedral of a woman –
this is my home and you are my church.
I am looking for a queen for my city.
I am looking for my children outside
in the high street. I can sit to listen
to whatever wherever I want and I won't
sit in the road – I don't like to ebb
when the traffic is good at moving all
by itself. I am learning
stillness which is only loving
each room of my house – the cluttered

kitchen-bathroom   the living room filled
with strangers next friday
night   the empty hall – and finding
my bedroom full of the women
I love and the men even
when they are print-out
portraits. that way
when I am entertaining I will be saying
exactly what I would say

Gravedigger

I walk to empty my head
down the road is a brush and I go looking
up up there is a brittle thin stick canopy
through the gaps drops some rain
and blackbird song and blank light and
my body bent, long arm and palm
open, under the brush I unearth a skull
here is a skull now
so much love too much
hold it up on my palm and recite
the line, I go back to
the house and google it to find
I found a domestic cat
skull in the underbrush

this world is vulgar

or just this small piece, I wash
the mud out of its empty eye
sockets and clean six small teeth and two
thicker fangs, I feel
its brittle blank white scalp and think
this could be any cat, my cat
runs under my feet
I scoop him up and he feels
like so much love, I smooth back his two ears the way
he seems to like being touched, I want
to say sorry sorry, in the garden
under a plant pot the skull
trembles off another piece
of mud

Alice Willitts was recently awarded the prize for shortest biog in the history of UEA Live: an accolade not to be tinkered with.

Author, poet, mother, gardener, designer, diseased, bereaved – did I mention she has great friends?

Who are you and why are you speaking on her behalf? And in italics too!

anotherkindofhappiness.wordpress.com

Dementia is not a squirrel

In-shrinking. Words to grow
my mind back. Burying the words is
a slosh in learning
              what language can talk of time
stopping.   The thought of it snags
in my brain parts and grinds out
no sequence, only the patter
of distant tyres on a rainy day
        at the prickly part of my neck
    what language can speak to the chair
          that doesn't know itself   under me
or the table mat that becomes   toast spread
thickly with   raspberry   glue
what is   language when it tumbles from my brain
to throat   crumpling thought   recycling
words I'd never say
        litters them, they.   They
are losing things careless buggers
              what's it for   when all the edges   of the people
    and the room   piantings are disoslving out of
thesmelves   crawling over   eahc other the faces
of my pepole   melting. Thaw is only
langauge when all the edges of the   peploe
and the door and the ojecbts are   disvlosing into each
other   over thesvselmes   melting   waht is
laaugnge wehn all the eegds of the plpoee and
the   patinigns   ilgnssdvoi ecah
oreht   faces crawling   with maggots revolting insects

The radio plays
'a squirrel's patchy memory is a tree's dream of a future'
dementia is not like a   squid   or a brush

Dying is not a climb but it's a close thing

sitting in   at your dying   protesting   women only
like lying down before the gate   long days and nights   as
harsh old shadow rat   whiskers the gentle folds of our
sleeping   mother and daughters   who keep time in breath
only   out   out   cauterise time   out   out   rotter
out   no   i don't go back   because (the memories)

at your dying   the only stars are in the sky   and a pale
exposed ridge ahead   forwards and towards   is the only path
our temerarious cortège (♀) falters   as a following storm sucks
high wisps into its mane   up the valley   and our belts start
humming   like bees singing   like we've picked up
swarming bees   speaking urgently of themselves

we're frozen in an eerie threnody   which fills the air
then bursts   pitch lightning   jaggers the path beneath our
silent feet   and to the siren song   little flints leap up like
hopeful salmon   going home   reckless hearts
for the keening is aeolian static   singing in our metal belts!

a jeremiad of bees   circles me still   and yes
you were luminous   like a blood transfusion   and I adored you
but   even in my dreams   I know you are no longer
not even in the mineral lights of stars

Strategy xi: just be

to sit together in silence   or gather together all the startled birds
from dawn   or visit closed corners of childhood   Familiar
the homesick letters   the rank wax floor-polish   the cool
green of wall-tiles on bruises   Familiar
she invites me to just be   I don't ask her   because that's not
why we're here   we talk about everything that isn't

Strategy vi: screaming with gulls

Baffled amusement and deep love
as he watches me shul barefoot
across the shivering sand

pink in a stripe of black swimming costume
to slip gracefully (would you believe it)
into that supine pain

The wild in me drawn   no
sucked   into the February sea

Strategy i: surrender

my heart is oily blue swallows   frantic to escape   birds
whose flight is grace   fall to earth   one   by
one   exhausted   broken

swift cockroaches carpet sorrow   muffle the impulse to
resist   miniature mouthful   by miniature mouthful   away

and my heart   stripped clean   by the many
tongues of grief   continues   more than less   to beat

\DART\not to paralyse\

the honeybee darts smartly from flower to flower   humming
as she goes   you are here only as a shadow is   and a skein
all undone   we work side by side, fingering the thread
following each knot to its end   to find another
     your old hands flutter   buffeted by unjust gusts and dart
away as you reach for mine   frustrated fingers calm to pick and
pull between yours   ours together   untangle the knotted silks
         an autumn spider   darts to paralyse the struggling
honeybee   spinning it over and under   a thick flow of silk
silk pouring from her thorax
         now you are contented   and sit with the sensible
spool filling your shrunk lap   *so so much* you say like a wide
eyed child stroking the nice feeling   my eyes dart off
and when I turn back   you've tangled in it again
          immobilised   confounded threads are
woven about your everyday purpose   you're so far away
I can't   reach you   even as I   hold you

Strategy vii: take a walk with laura mvula

when my noon shadow   is longer than the tree   that scaffolds
the frost blades   yes go   but hold me first   gilded
squint of a woman   and   leg blind

December composts days
   to let us fall
   to be litter
in the briefest armful   and shelters us   sharpest in the light

The argument against

No
daughter, if you were to run after me
I would fly at you
with pan handles and brooms.
daughter, if you tried to stay
I would shout outside your room
at unreasonable hours, interrupt
your phonecalls and shoo you.
daughter, if you tried to hug me
I would smack your sweet face.
            I forbid you to come here.

                                        Night
                    I would just slip down beside you
                    and wash my hands in you. Lean in
                      to your too willing heart, *sillygirl*,
                              press my lips and drink
                                in lush butterflykisses
                                on your face, nose-rub
                            eskimokisses to soak in
                      your milky breath, *darlingirl*,
                    and with the tips of my fingers
                        fill in your delicate eyebrows
                              and stroke the wisps
                              from your forehead

Morning
I will rend and scream and I will tidy
violently. I will suck sour bitters
when you come in and I will plead
beg, if I have to. If you
run after me, daughter
if oh my Grace my Comfort my Soul my
Hope my Faith my Mercy my Own my
oh please, *make her live*

Starting over

First: showing up.

Tail tucked, snickering,

to dance till I am sodden

with dew and the small

yellow butterflies come

in their hundreds.

Clothe me.

Shame won't

be held

like diamonds

but water.

Bloodied jaw   steady

hold this slack blush pear

like a newborn pup.

Here   I am

tasteless and wretched

but   here.

Acknowledgements

Thanks are due to the School of Literature, Drama and Creative Writing at UEA in partnership with Egg Box Publishing for making the UEA MA Creative Writing anthologies possible.

Tiffany Atkinson, Trezza Azzopardi, Stephen Benson, Clare Connors, Andrew Cowan, Alison Donnell, Giles Foden, Sarah Gooderson, Rachel Hore, Kathryn Hughes, Thomas Karshan, Philip Langeskov, Timothy Lawrence-Cave, Jean McNeil, Paul Mills, Jeremy Noel-Tod, Denise Riley, Lisa Robertson, Sophie Robinson, Helen Smith, Rebecca Stott, Henry Sutton, George Szirtes, Matt Taunton, Ian Thomson, Steve Waters, Julia Webb, Naomi Wood.

Nathan Hamilton at UEA Publishing Project, and Emily Benton.

Editorial Committee:
    Justus Flair
    Faye Holder
    Laurence Hardy
    Yin F Lim
    Aaron O'Farrell
    Sureshkumar Pasupula Sekar
    Saloni Prasad
    George Utton

Thanks go to Craig Barker, Kat Franceska, Iona May, Max Bowden, Rachel Goodman, Anna Cathenka, and Alice Willitts for copy-editing. John Anthony for film-making.

With grateful thanks to all the funders who support the scholarships that support our poets, in particular:
    The Ink Sweat and Tears Scholarship
    The Birch Family Scholarship
    The Bryan Heiser Memorial Bursary

UEA Creative Writing MA Anthology: Poetry, 2018

First published by Egg Box Publishing, 2018
part of UEA Publishing Project Ltd.

Cover image by Laurence Hardy, 2018.
From the poem 'In Parentheses'.

A CIP record for this book is available from the British Library.
Printed and bound in the UK by Imprint Digital.

Designed by Emily Benton.
emilybentonbookdesigner.co.uk

Proofread by Sarah Gooderson.
Distributed by NEN International
10 Thornby Road Plymouth
PL6 7PPT +44(0)1752 202 3102
e.cservs@nbninternational.com

ISBN: 978-1-911343-42-4